Letters to My Little Sisters

Letters to My Little Sisters

JAMI LYN
BUCHANAN

Illustrated
by
Wendy Talbot

Regal
Books

A Division of GL Publications
Ventura, California, U.S.A.

Rights for publishing this book in other languages are contracted by Gospel
Literature International foundation (GLINT). GLINT also provides technical
help for the adaptation, translation, and publishing of Bible study resources
and books in more than 100 languages worldwide. For further information,
contact GLINT, Post Office Box 6688, Ventura, California 93006, U.S.A.,
or the publisher.

Library of Congress Cataloging in Publication Data applied for.

This book is dedicated to
Shawna Sundstrom
and
Jeni Amsler
the two girls who were
just like little sisters
to me.

Contents

Foreword

Did you ever go someplace where you've never been before and wind up all by yourself? Alone?! It can be pretty frightening depending upon what you do, what you think, and how you feel about your situation.

Some people go nuts! They worry, they make themselves scared, depressed, angry, or just feel sorry for themselves. But they don't do anything about their predicament!

Others think, "I'm lost; what am I going to do about it?" or they find somebody who can help.

Maybe you're at a place in your life where you feel a little lost or alone. With all the changes happening inside of you and decisions and discoveries you are making, it could be a little scary!

Scary, unless you had a friend, somebody special who is a little bit older and wiser—like a big sister.

I'd like you to meet a friend of mine who is special, creative, and has a lot of good things to say. She'll answer a lot of questions you might have, and she doesn't put you down for the way you feel.

You'll get to know her real well as you read her letters, because she writes very openly, honestly, and intimately about herself and the friends she's met and learned from along the way.

I'm glad I took the time to get to know Jami, and I think you will be glad you did too.

Dave Hopkins

Forest Home

Preface

I became a Christian as a very little girl, but my real commitment came at the end of junior high. I realized that adolescence is the most impressionable time in life. So I began working with the junior highers in my church to help them see that there is another life-style than the one the world has to offer. I had so much to share with the girls but seldom had the opportunity to teach on subjects just for them. So I began to write a book.

Each chapter of the book is written as a letter that deals with subjects an adolescent girl might encounter in life or might be curious about. As I wrote about each subject I tried to relate to the feelings they have, share my experiences on the subject, and then show them how God would want them to handle themselves in that area. At the end of each chapter are Scriptures and explanations that relate to the subject and how they can apply to the girls' lives.

Self-Image

My Little Sisters,

Have you ever looked at someone and wished you could be just like him or her? It's common. I often see people that I want to be like in one way or another.

Think of all the things about yourself that you would change if you could. I'll bet that if I asked you to make a list of your good qualities and a list of your bad qualities, the two lists would end up being very different in size. You would probably put your good qualities on a piece of paper the size of a postage stamp and ask for a roll of toilet paper on which to list your bad qualities. Mind you, no one is that imbalanced! But that is how we tend to view ourselves.

We girls seem to be our own worst critics. And teen and pre-teen girls seem to be the very worst! Having a bad self-image is a disease that runs rampant among them but certainly isn't limited to them. Everyone struggles with his or her self-image.

Girls think everyone is better than they are! They hate themselves for the smallest things—from an uneven part in their hair to how weirdly their little toe curls under. Silly, isn't it? But I've seen girls run out of a room because of embarrassment over such things.

So how do you improve your self-image? I wish I could tell you to follow steps one through ten and then guarantee you a great self-image. If only it were that easy! But it's not.

We need to learn to search for the good in ourselves instead of always looking at the bad. Make a list of all your good qualities. Don't leave anything out! Be sure to include how comfortably your nose fits on the front of your face (providing it is on the front of your face, of course). List everything!

But even before you start the list, try to look at yourself through God's eyes. Try to see God's image of you. Wow! What a beautiful creature you can be, inside and out!

If you are a Christian (oh, I hope you are), God sees Jesus Christ in you. "I have been crucified with Christ and I no longer live, but Christ lives in me" (Gal. 2:20). You have Christ in you! Just think, all of the perfection lives right inside of you! That's what God sees when He looks at you.

Psalm 139:13-16 tells about God's forming of us while we were still in our mother's wombs. Verse 14 says, "I praise you because I am fearfully and wonderfully made." Did you hear that? You are wonderfully made. I am willing to say that you are wonderful! Yeah, you! And by the way, that verse reminds us that we should give thanks to God for that fact. When was the last time you thanked God for how wonderfully He made you? That long? Well, do it now. Say thanks.

Did I hear one of you say what I thought I heard you say? You aren't thankful for how God made you? You don't think He did such a red-hot job? You think that even God is entitled to one mistake and you're it, that when God made you He was playing a practical joke on the world? Boy, are you brave! I would never have the nerve to tell God He has bad taste. God doesn't make mistakes. No matter how poor your self-image is, God's image of you is still wonderful.

"But Jami," you say, "look at my face. It looks like someone put it together with an egg beater. I'm so ugly that my mom asked if she could have her money back when she first saw me!" Not all of us can look like Miss America. Sure, there will always be people who are more attractive than we are, and we will always want to look great. But being beautiful isn't all it's cracked up to be. Sometimes it can even be more of a curse. Think of the prettiest girl at school. What do people say about her? Rumors are spread about her, people think she's stuck-up, and guys ask her out for her looks without caring about the person inside. How would you like that kind of treatment from people you didn't even know?

I like the way I look. I fall into the average category. There is rarely any doubt in my mind why people spend time with me. It's because they like being around the person I am inside, not for what I look like on the outside. Thank God!

All of the makeup in the world isn't going to make you beautiful if you're ugly on the inside.

There's nothing wrong with a little makeup to highlight your natural beauty. A little blush or mascara can work wonders in perking up your face. Teenage girls seem to have tons of fun putting on makeup and playing with their hair, and you can do the same. (Don't tell anyone, but my hair isn't naturally curly. I'd look like a Q-Tip if I didn't have my permanent.)

But, outward beauty is only temporary. Though one pimple on the end of your nose might appear to ruin everything, the inside remains the same no matter how many pimples you get. So it is important to develop the person on the inside into someone of value. I don't know the specific qualities that make you special. But I do know that you are special to God. Why? Because the Body of Christ (the church) needs you. First Corinthians 12 tells us that in the Body of Christ there are many part and all of those parts are absolutely necessary. That means that even you are necessary.

Have you ever felt dumb or not quite as spiritual as someone else? I feel that way at times. There are people who seem to have the entire Bible memorized. Several of my friends have gone to Christian colleges to study things like Greek and theology. There are times when I feel very inadequate around them. But I shouldn't! I may not be able to recite the book of Genesis, but I can share my love for Christ and show that love to others through my friendliness and hospitality.

You are absolutely necessary and important to the Body of Christ, too. Use the gifts the Holy Spirit has given you to benefit the Body of Christ. It's not complete without you.

We all need compliments and encouragement from others. When you finally realize how wonderful you are (and you are wonderful), you will be able to accept compliments graciously because you'll know that it is God in you that makes you special. Then you can help others discover how wonderful they are by pointing out their strengths and special qualities.

I think that I have a healthy image of myself. But I didn't always. I used to want to be more popular than I was. And I was always liking guys who didn't like me back. That lowered the image I had of myself. On top of everything else, I was the middle child in our family. It seemed as if my older sister got more privileges than I did, and my younger brother never had as much responsibility as I had. Sometimes I felt that no one cared. But I guess that's normal for all middle children. Older children should have more privileges. They are probably more mature and can handle privileges better. Younger kids shouldn't have to take on more responsibility than they are ready for. I see that now, but back then, when I was a kid, it just didn't seem fair.

There was one situation in my life which was a major factor in developing my self-image into what it is today. It was a hard lesson to learn, but I thank God that He allowed me to experience it. While I was in college I became engaged to a young man. I thought he was the most wonderful man in the world. I was eager to be his wife and make him happy in any way I could. But soon he tried to mold and shape me into what he wanted me to be instead of loving me just the way I was. Because I wanted to make him happy, I tried to be what he wanted me to be. But I wasn't being the real Jami, and I wasn't happy. When the engagement was finally broken I was more relieved than hurt. It felt so good to be myself again instead of trying to be someone I wasn't meant to be. I felt so free. I know there are areas in my life that need improvement. God will take care of those things when He's ready. But in general I feel that He has done a pretty good job on me so far! I love being me!

Love being you! It's so much easier than trying to be someone else!

Jami

James 2:8—"Love your neighbor as yourself." *How can you love your neighbor if you don't love yourself?*

Proverbs 23:7—"For as he thinks within himself, so he is" (NASB). *You are what you believe you are. Believe you are wonderful. God does!*

Psalm 139:14—"I am fearfully and wonderfully made." *God says so. Be in agreement with Him.*

1 Corinthians 12:27—"Now you are the body of Christ, and each one of you is a part of it." *You are important to the Body of Christ. You are at your best when you are fulfilling your position in the Body of Christ.*

Matthew 10:30—"And even the very hairs of your head are all numbered." *You are so valuable to God that He even keeps track of how many hairs you have on your head. That's valuable!*

Ephesians 2:8,9—"For it is by grace you have been saved, through faith—and this not from yourselves, it is the gift of God—not by works . . . . " *We don't have to do anything to get God to love us. He loves us just the way we are.*

Popularity

My Little Sisters,

*Everyone wants to be popular. But not everyone
can be. I wanted to be popular when I was in junior
high school so I did all the things that the popular
girls did. But now that I look back on some of those
things they seem absolutely ridiculous. For instance,
one of the things that all the popular girls did was to
wear animal print bikini underwear. Gym class was
your big chance to show off your underwear and
there would be every kind of animal of the jungle
running around the locker room. Zebras, tigers,
snakes, and the like. If you didn't wear fancy bikini
underwear you were a real jerk. Pants were worn
super tight back then. So it was really cool to be
able to see your bikini panty line through them. If
you didn't wear the right kind of underwear you
were not accepted. Can you believe that?*

*For the guys, being cool was even more
obvious. They wore boxer shorts and let them stick
out of the tops of their pants. Or if they were
wearing shorts, they let their underwear hang down
almost to their knees. Can you imagine judging a
person by the kind of underwear he or she wears?*

*Within a week of starting junior high everyone
knew who the popular people were. Annette was
the most popular girl. She had long brown hair and*

the cutest clothes of any girl on campus. The rest of us used to push each other aside so that we could stand next to her. All the guys liked her too. But of course she only liked the cutest and most popular guys. The whole crowd of popular people were always getting into trouble. It turns out that they were involved in drugs and alcohol. Most of them didn't even finish high school. I saw Annette at a park when she was about 16. She had cut her beautiful hair and was rip-roaring drunk. She was swearing up a storm at the guy she was with, and to make things even worse she was pregnant. Suddenly, being popular didn't seem so important.

I didn't fit in very well with that crowd of people. So by the time I was in high school I started to hang around the cheerleaders. They were all nice girls who got fairly good grades, never did anything terribly wrong, and dated the guys involved in sports. I didn't date very much in high school but I always wanted to be like the cheerleaders. After a while they gave in to peer pressures and started doing the wrong things in order to remain part of the crowd.

I went to a party with them once. They were all getting drunk, smoking, and making out with guys who weren't even their boyfriends. It really upset me because one of the guys they were all taking turns kissing was the guy I liked. That cut deep. I didn't approve of the things they did, and they didn't like having me around if I wasn't going to participate. So, needless to say, I was no longer accepted as part of that crowd. For the rest of my high school days I wasn't very popular.

I'm not going to pretend with you: it wasn't easy. Many weekends I stayed home and watched "The Mary Tyler Moore Show." I wanted to be popular but to me it just wasn't worth it to do things I believed were wrong in order to have a lot of friends.

That's what being popular is, isn't it? Having a lot of friends? But think about it. Do popular people really have that many friends, or do they have a lot of acquaintances? How deep are their friendships? Out of all the popular people I hung around with not one proved to be a good or close friend to me. They were always concerned with doing what would help them maintain their popularity.

And when I look at those same girls now I see that none of them finished college, one of them had to get married because she was pregnant, a couple lived with their boyfriends and then broke up. One is considering divorce but knows she will have difficulty raising her three children on her own if she goes through with it. Another spends more money on drugs than she does on her children's doctor bills. Those girls aren't even 25 years old yet, and already their lives are a total mess.

What about you? Where is popularity going to get you once you're out of high school? Being a cheerleader doesn't get you a good job, and it doesn't qualify you for college. It is far more important to develop skills and a knowledge of yourself that will have lasting value. And develop the kind of deep friendships that will endure forever.

27

Don't aim for popularity and only end up with many acquaintances. Be a person with the kind of friendships that last forever.

Look at the example Jesus sets for us. Jesus was not popular with the rulers of His day; He didn't go along with the crowd. In fact, He spoke out against what those leaders were doing. They disliked Him so much that they tried to kill Him. But Jesus did have a small band of intimate friends—the 12 apostles. Out of that group of 12 there were three to whom He was closest. Jesus never compromised what He believed in order to win the crowds. He set the standards. I encourage you to do the same. Being popular has no lasting value. Being yourself does.

Jami

Proverbs 18:24—"A man of many companions may come to ruin, but there is a friend who sticks closer than a brother." *Having lots of friends can cause us to come to ruin. Instead, we should be trying to develop close friendships.*

1 John 2:15—"Do not love the world or anything in the world. If anyone loves the world, the love of the Father is not in him." *Don't let becoming popular in this world pull you away from your love for God. Realize that popularity is only temporary. Set your mind on eternal things.*

Peer
Pressure

My Little Sisters,

I am the world's biggest chicken! I hardly ever got into trouble when I was young, mainly because I was afraid of getting caught. I've never been drunk. I've never had a cigarette. I've never taken drugs. I guess that from some people's point of view, I'm a very boring person. But I also don't bear any terrible scars from things that I've done wrong.

I will tell you, however, one little story. When I was at junior high camp my friends and I went over to the high school camp. My girl friend liked Mark, one of the guys there. Once we arrived, Mark and his roommates invited us to go inside their cabin. Well, as I told you, I'm a chicken! All of my girl friends went inside the cabin—but I didn't, because the boys' cabins were off-limits to the girls. Sure enough, my friends got caught. When the dean of our camp found out, he put them all on restriction— including me! He figured that if I hung around those kids I must have been in on the mischief too. Well, we finally got it all straightened out and I was taken off restriction.

That is a pretty innocent story, but it speaks clearly about a number of things. Even though we may be innocent, we are still judged by what our friends do. It sounds rather unfair, but at the same time it does make sense. I think every intelligent adult knows what a strong influence friends can have. That's why peer pressure is so easy to give in to.

What exactly is peer pressure? It is the influence of those around us (our friends and those of our age group) to follow their standards of conduct and way of thinking, and to adopt their value systems.

Each day the influence of your peers affects the kind of clothes you wear, the music you listen to, the gossip you hear and spread, whether or not you accept outsiders into your group, the ways in which you try to act cool or show disrespect for authority, and your attitudes toward swearing, drinking, smoking, and premarital sex. Sometimes peer pressure can be a good thing, but often it is not. The attitudes that the majority of your peers have in these areas can be very damaging to you and your reputation, not to mention that they are often completely opposite of what God wants you to do.

Handling peer pressure isn't easy, especially for someone of your age. I know how important it is for you to be accepted by others. But it is up to you to decide whether you want to go along with what everyone else does in order to be accepted or if you want to do what is right and best for you regardless of what your peers think. I hope you choose the latter.

One way to handle peer pressure is to start by stating what you believe, then sticking to your guns. Don't be afraid to go against the crowd. If others don't accept you for what you believe, then I would begin questioning their friendship. Talk to someone whom you admire and respect, perhaps a person a little younger than your parents. We have several college-age students who work with our youth group at church. If your church does too, try talking with one of them. I know they would love to help.

Another way to handle peer pressure is by being selective when you first choose your friends. Look for those who will have a positive influence on you, people your parents approve of, those who will help make you a stronger person.

But the most important way to handle peer pressure is to turn to God for the strength you need to withstand worldly influences. You know that God is going to accept you no matter how different you are from the crowd. He made you to be an individual. He loves you just the way you are.

Jami

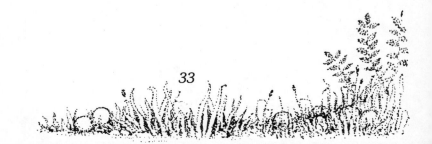

Ephesians 2:10—"For we are God's workmanship, created in Christ Jesus to do good works, which God prepared in advance for us to do." *We were created to do good things. Don't let the crowd talk you into doing things that you know are wrong.*

Romans 12:1,2—"Therefore, I urge you, brothers, in view of God's mercy, to offer your bodies as living sacrifices, holy and pleasing to God—which is your spiritual worship. Do not conform any longer to the pattern of this world, but be transformed by the renewing of your mind. Then you will be able to test and approve what God's will is—his good, pleasing and perfect will." *God wants us to be different from the world, not just like it.*

1 Corinthians 15:33—"Bad company ruins good morals" (RSV). *Keeping company with the wrong crowd will make a good person weak.*

Friends

My Little Sisters,

When I think about the topic of friendship, the first thing I want to do is tell you about a few of my friends. I have several friends but only a handful who are extra special. Because many of my girl friends are away at college or busy with new jobs or boyfriends, we don't get to see each other as much as we'd like. But even though we don't see much of each other we still share special love and memories of slumber parties, camps, and long phone conversations. We've laughed together and cried together. We share gifts at birthdays and Christmas or for no reason. One of my girl friends even brought me flowers. It was incredibly special.

My close friend, Fabi, just got married. The two of us had a blast sharing thoughts on men and marriage and looking through Brides *magazine during her engagement. Fabi is special to me because she is so sweet and keeps me laughing. Sometimes that can be the best medicine in the world.*

Some of my other close friends are guys. They've been like brothers to me. Eric has helped me grow in my ministry more than any other person. He's stretched me and challenged me to do things I never would have done on my own. Dennis

lives right across the street and he is available to talk at any time of the day or night. I can always count on the fact that he will send me flowers on my birthday. We will be friends even when we're old and rickety. Another dear friend whom I've gotten to know quite well in the last year is Johnny. He helps me see some of my shortcomings and work to improve them. It's good to have friends who help you grow. It has meant so much to me to have each one of these guys in my life. I seek their advice constantly; I value their wisdom and concern.

My friendships don't stop with people my own age. Pete and Marlene are a couple in our church whom I love and respect very much and who are old enough to be my parents. I used to go over to their house just to talk and visit, and they opened their doors to me as if I were one of their own children. And I even have friends who are old enough to be my grandparents. The Crosiers were my next-door neighbors while I was growing up. I love talking to them about anything and everything. They see things from a completely different point of view than I do—one that reflects the wisdom of age and experience. I love them like family.

But there is one group of people that has shown me more unconditional love and friendship than any other. That is the youth group from my church. In 1979 I had to move away from home for about 10 months. I got more letters and prayers from those kids than from friends my own age. Now that I'm back home they've continued to show me their love and concern. In a youth group as big as the one I work with it is easy to get too busy to spend the time I'd like to with special girls. Amy is one girl who, no matter how much or how little time I spend with her, puts a letter, note, or poem in my hand when she sees me. What a special love, what a special friend.

God, in His Word, doesn't tell us what to expect of our friends, but instead tells us how to be a good friend. And, of course, Jesus Christ is the perfect example of a good friend. So let's talk about what we should be like as friends.

How good a friend are you? Do you give only if someone gives first? Or do your friends think of you as a valuable, giving person? The Bible says, "Be devoted to one another in brotherly love" (Rom. 12:10). Do you try your hardest to be giving to your friends or do you take advantage of them? I encourage you to do all you can for your friends. Make them feel special and important through little gifts, notes, and prayers.

Proverbs 17:17 tells us, "A friend loves at all times." How about you? Are you a close friend only when things go well for your friends? Friends especially need one another when troubles come. School and family problems can be very painful. You may not know the perfect words to say to take away a friend's pain, but you can stick by him or her no matter what. Don't be a conditional friend. Love your friends always, through good times and bad.

Another way you can be a good friend is to refrain from gossiping. "A gossip separates close friends," says Proverbs 16:28. Ouch! Do you gossip about your friends behind their backs? Do you listen to gossip about them or do you try to stop it? Gossip can cause the best of friends to part. It's hard for your friends to trust you when you've betrayed their confidence. Can your friends trust you when they tell you a secret?

Good friends are also willing to be honest when the truth hurts. Have you ever asked for a friend's advice or opinion on something you've done? Like, "Do you think I'm overweight?" And the reply is, "No, you look fine, just fine." But you know that you are fat. In fact, you're so fat that your pants won't zip up and your flab rolls out of the top. In Proverbs 27:6 we read, "Wounds from a friend are better than kisses from an enemy" (TLB). It's difficult to speak the truth in love to a friend when it's not what that person wants to hear. But according to Scripture, that's what true friendship is all about.

Not too long ago one of my best friends and I disagreed about something. Instead of talking to her about it, I avoided the subject and began to avoid her. I allowed a small conflict to mushroom into something gigantic. When it was all over I felt awful because I hadn't gone to my friend right away with my concerns. I wasn't being a good friend, one who would be willing to lovingly confront the other person.

Proverbs 27:17 tells us, "As iron sharpens iron, so one man sharpens another." Your friends should be better people because of their contact with you. Do you encourage them and pray for them? Do you help them to become more mature and responsible?

Are you giving them good advice and setting a good example for them? Or do you get your friends into trouble because of your influence? Iron sharpens iron! Do you wear your friends down and make them dull, or are they sharp because you are their friend?

I've had friends whom I have loved so much that I wanted to do something special for them. Presents were never enough. I've learned that the most valuable things I can give my friends are prayers and words of encouragement. I can tell them how important and wonderful they are through cards or notes. Then I ask my very big God to guide their way and draw them closer to Himself. When you appreciate your friends be sure to tell them so. Show them your love.

I want to tell you about my very best friend! I love Him very, very much. And He loves me even more. Some of you girls probably think I'm talking about my boyfriend. Wrong! I'm talking about Jesus!

Again in Proverbs it says, "There is a friend who sticks closer than a brother" (18:24). Hey, we're talking close! I have spent all my life with my big sister. We've suffered through ups and downs together, and we've grown closer and closer as we have gotten older. But Jesus is even closer than a blood relative.

He says, "I no longer call you servants, because a servant does not know his master's business. Instead, I have called you friends, for everything that I learned from my Father I have made known to you" (John 15:15).

Finally, John 15:13 says, "Greater love has no one than this, that one lay down his life for his friends." Jesus is the only one who has ever done that for me. And Jesus died for you too. He loves you more than any human being ever could. He wants to be your best friend. Let Him!

Proverbs 22:24,25—"Do not make friends with a hot-tempered man, do not associate with one easily angered, or you may learn his ways and get yourself ensnared." *Be careful in choosing your friends because you may become like them.*

Romans 12:10—"Be devoted to one another in brotherly love." *Some ways to start: send notes to your friends, do something special for their birthdays, call them when they're sick.*

Proverbs 18:24—"There is a friend who sticks closer than a brother." *That friend is Jesus. He's waiting to be your friend.*

Hebrews 10:24—"And let us consider how we may spur one another on toward love and good deeds." *Encourage your friends to grow spiritually.*

Modesty

My Little Sisters,

I could just cringe at the image that enters some people's minds when they hear the phrase "nice Christian girl"! Picture this . . . her bathing suit is a two-piece—and I don't mean a bikini. The top is an elbow-length sleeve with a turtle neck. It's really "swell." It buttons up the front and only a rebellious girl would consider unbottoning the first button. The bottom is equally attractive. It is loose-fitting and extends below the knee. Heaven forbid that it should be above the knee! The total suit is usually a dull color, but those Christian girls who enjoy being in the height of fashion make it out of a print consisting of oversized flowers. Heads turn as this "nice Christian girl" walks down the beach in her lovely suit. But it's not because she has a knockout tan, believe me.

The bathing suit I just described is certainly modest. But it's awfully ridiculous. It's ugly too! (I hope your suit isn't like the one I just described!) Besides, it wouldn't be at all functional for the beach or for swimming.

Then there are girls at the other end of the spectrum. My Sunday School girls and I spent a lot of time at the beach last summer. We saw some real humdinger bathing suits, with barely enough material to cover up the vital areas. Again you could see heads turn as the girls wearing those bathing suits walked down the beach, and again it wasn't their deep, dark tans that people were staring at. The girls we saw in those bathing suits had very little modesty. I hope your bathing suit falls somewhere between those two extremes.

Why should we, as Christians, be modest? Because a Christian's body is the temple of the Holy Spirit. We should treat that temple with pride and respect. Through it we reflect Jesus Christ to others. We need to set a good example.

Some questions to ask yourself as you dress or shop for clothes are, how would I feel if Jesus saw me dressed in that outfit? Would I be embarrassed if He saw me? Or would I feel comfortable having Him right there with me dressed the way I am?

Okay, let's set some standards for dressing modestly. Since I've already mentioned bathing suits let's start with those. I was thrilled when one-piece bathing suits came back in style. They are great! You can dive into the pool without your top falling off and without you falling out! There's nothing wrong with a two-piece, but don't plan on being very active in one. No matter how careful you are, accidents do happen. Wear a bathing suit that covers up all of the important places. Be comfortable when you wear your suit, not self-conscious.

Summer seems to be the notorious season for lack of modesty. What do you think when you see a girl whose shorts are so short that her underwear and fanny hang out? EEEEECH! But even I have been guilty of that one. So here's a little test to keep that from happening. After you have your shorts on, bend way over. Check the mirror or have a friend let you know what's exposed. If there's anything hanging out, then change your shorts!

Some other things to avoid when you dress are tops that are so low-cut that your bra shows, clothes that are so tight that you can't grab a pinch of material, and clothes cut in a way that lets your bra straps hang out! By the way, as you begin to grow into a woman a bra becomes an absolute necessity to ensure modesty.

Modesty doesn't mean being ugly or out of style. But it does mean that you may have to alter some of the things that are in fashion in order to remain modest. Who are you dressing to please? Your girl friends . . . guys . . . or God? Remember, clothes don't make the person—it's the heart inside that's important.

1 Timothy 2:9,10—"I also want women to dress modestly, with decency and propriety, not with braided hair or gold or pearls or expensive clothes, but with good deeds, appropriate for women who profess to worship God." *This verse tells us to make modesty and discretion the first things we put on when we dress ourselves. We should be noticed for the good things we do, rather than for what we are wearing.*

1 Peter 3:3,4—"Your beauty should not come from outward adornment, such as braided hair and the wearing of gold jewelry and fine clothes. Instead, it should be that of your inner self, the unfading beauty of a gentle and quiet spirit, which is of great worth in God's sight." *Wearing a fashionable new dress or doing your hair a new way is a lot of fun. Today's fashions will pass away but the quality of a gentle and quiet spirit won't. It is precious in the sight of God. Be sure that your character is lovely. The latest fashions won't complete your beauty. Your beauty needs to begin inside.*

Boys

My Little Sisters,

As I sit down to write to you about my favorite subject, I can't help but think of all the time I have spent talking about boys. It seems like that is all we girls ever talked about at slumber parties, camp, school, church, and especially on the telephone. Boys are definitely one of the most interesting things in life.

At your age there are some big differences between boys and girls. Have you noticed that a lot of the girls are bigger than the boys? Or that girls seem to act more mature than the boys do? That's because girls reach puberty sooner than guys do, physically and mentally. Girls mature more rapidly. Eventually the boys catch up, but until then the difference is the pits!

My feeling is that relationships with boys should be taken pretty seriously. Boys are God's creation too and not something to be taken advantage of. One of the first things we need to remember is that Christian boys are our brothers in Christ. We have to answer to God for anything we do that involves them. We should keep from doing anything that hinders their growing relationship with God. No matter how dumb, ugly, or squirrelly they can be we still have to love them like brothers.

Some of the neatest, most long-lasting

51

friendships I have are with guys. I have learned so very much from them, and I hope they have learned a lot from me. I have enjoyed giving them a hand from time to time in things that needed a woman's touch. As I write this letter my three most special male friends are engaged to be married. I even get to be in one of the weddings. I have enjoyed spending time getting to know their future wives and already feel like they are my good friends too.

Guys can be extra special as friends. You can be yourself when you're with a guy who is a close friend. It's like having a brother your own age. He'll stick up for you, give you the male point of view (very valuable when you want to know what makes guys tick), and if he's really special he can be a strong shoulder to cry on when you're feeling low.

My little sisters, I just can't begin to tell you how valuable special guy friends can be. So often I hear girls refer to a guy that they've been dating as "just a friend." They make it sound like the relationship is so empty. And perhaps, because those girls want something that they think is more important than friendship, it is empty. Boyfriends come and go, but friends can remain friends forever. Don't think that just because all the other girls have boyfriends that you should have one too. Appreciate the friendships you have with guys and be satisfied with them. Sometimes God allows those friendships to grow into more, but not until it is time.

"But Jami, I want to hear about boys as boyfriends!" Okay, fine! Read my next letter to you. It's completely devoted to dating!

Jami

Proverbs 17:17—"A friend loves at all times." *Love your guy friends at all times. Sometimes their male friends aren't very sympathetic about problem situations and as a girl you can really help them out.*

Romans 12:10—"Be devoted to one another in brotherly love." *Just because a guy isn't your boyfriend doesn't mean you can't do special things for him. Do favors for him! Be devoted to the friendship you have between you.*

Dating

My Little Sisters,

One of the things I most looked forward to when I became a teenager was dating. I could hardly wait! It was going to be such a big deal. Well, it still is. I still use the suggestions I am about to pass on to you because I still get excited when I get to go out with a guy I think is special!

I tried to think of questions that you might have about dating or about what to do on your first date. So, Ready! Set! Go!

Why should I date?

To be a balanced person you need to develop socially. It's important to learn to handle yourself with people. And besides that, guys are fun to get to know and be with. But don't feel like you have to date just because everyone else does. Wait until you feel comfortable with the idea.

How old should I be when I start dating?

Your parents are the ones who should decide the answer to that question. They know what's best for you and when you're ready. I have seen so many girls start dating before they were ready and who made very immature decisions about the kind of guys they went out with or the places they went.

My parents allowed me to date when I turned 15. I was so excited about being able to date I could hardly stand it. So, I went out with the first guy who asked me. I didn't really care who he was, I just wanted to go on a date! Because I didn't take the time to consider whether or not we had anything in common I had a terrible time. The worst part was that after I went out with him I couldn't get rid of him. It was a long time after that before I went on another date.

My friend, Dave, was disappointed to find that there wasn't anything in the Bible written specifically on the subject of dating. He said that if there were, it would come from the book of "Frustrations" and it would read something like this: "We should not be like the hungry bear who runs around searching for food. No matter what he finds, good or bad, he eats it. Instead, we should be like the farmer who works diligently in his field each day and waits patiently for harvesttime when the grain is at its best." Do you understand what he is saying? Don't go out with a guy just because you're dying to date, but wait patiently and improve yourself until the right person comes along and makes the effort worthwhile.

What kind of guys should I go out with?

Only you can answer the specifics of that question because you know your likes and dislikes. You will probably have the most fun with a guy you have a few things in common with. Something really important to consider is the question of whether or not the guy is a Christian. If he is, that's great! You already have much in common. You can have an extra depth to your relationship that you won't have with someone who doesn't share your love for Christ. I suggest that you limit your dating to Christian guys. Their moral standards should be high and you will have fewer problems with sexual temptation. Don't get me wrong, Christian guys aren't perfect; they are human too. But if you and your date are both Christians then you are both accountable to God for what goes on in your relationship.

Don't hesitate to ask your friends for their opinions about the guy you like or the guy who has just asked you out. Friends are good at giving honest answers. Sometimes when guys ask us out we are so impressed with what good taste they have in women that we forget that they may not be the kind of guys we're really interested in.

Your parents are important too when it comes to checking out a guy. If they like him then they may give you a little extra freedom and responsibility in dating. Parents can be very critical because nothing is ever good enough for their little girl! They know you better than anyone else, so listen to their opinions. You can bet they are going to be very valuable.

What kind of guys shouldn't I date?

Guys who act like jerks, fools, idiots, slobs,

goons, nerds . . . . But you can't always tell those things right away. Maybe after a date or two you'll be able to figure it out.

Suppose a guy shows up an hour later than the arranged time and he's wearing old grubby, greasy clothes and he stinks! Ugh! He may have a good excuse, and then again he may not! You took the time to get ready and look your best for him. He should at least do the same for you. Punctuality is a form of courtesy. Let's hope that the guys you choose to go out with are polite.

Don't date a guy who doesn't respect you or your parents. I hope you wouldn't date a guy who goes against your parents' rules regarding curfew or off-limits places (drive-in movies, drinking parties). If you are ever in a situation that you know is wrong or that your parents wouldn't approve of, ask the young man to take you home. If he won't do that, then call Mom or Dad to come to the rescue. They will be glad to do it.

Where should I go on dates?

If your intention is to get to know a guy, then a movie really isn't a very good place to go. You don't get to talk to each other. Public places are good. Roller skating, miniature golfing, and church activities are all great for a date. They are even more fun when you double- or triple-date. The more, the merrier! It's all fun stuff and gives you the opportunity to learn more about the person you are dating.

I would strongly advise against going to dark romantic places. What you've heard about the drive-in theatre is all true. Don't allow yourself to get into a situation that may lead to trouble.

How should I dress?

Well, common sense tells you not to wear a formal to go roller skating. Wear something that you feel comfortable in and that is appropriate for the occasion. You may even ask the guy you're going out with what kind of clothes you should wear. It's kind of embarrassing to be too dressed up or wearing something that is not dressy enough.

Take time preparing yourself for this date. An hour or so before the guy picks you up should give you enough time. (Three weeks is not necessary!) You may even want to tidy up the living room a bit for him. And maybe you could do a couple of extra special things to yourself to impress him. Perfume is always a nice touch. you may even want to curl your hair or wear a new barrette. All of these things say that you think he's special.

A while ago I had a date for the first time with a guy I thought was extra special. If he only knew how much time I spent getting ready for that date there would have been no doubt in his mind just how special I thought he was. He wasn't going to pick me up until noon on Saturday. So how much time do you think I spent getting ready for that date? Two hours? Three hours? I started getting ready at five o'clock Friday night!

I cleaned my apartment from top to bottom. I

even waxed the floors and washed the windows. I was going to be cooking dinner for him, so I prepared everything in advance. Then I washed my hair, plucked my eyebrows, shaved my legs, and curled my hair. (Miss America, eat your heart out!) I couldn't have looked any better if I had tried. When he came to pick me up he commented about how clean my apartment looked. I batted my eyelashes and thanked him for the compliment—never letting him know how hard I worked to get it that way.

What should I talk about?

I just hate those awkward moments during which you just don't know what to say. I have a little game I play that helps. I call it the "Fungame." All it takes is two people who have good imaginations and want to get to know each other. The game is played like this: Make up a question that wouldn't come up in normal conversation such as, "What would you do if you had a million dollars?" or "If you could live anywhere in the world, where would you like to live?" The guy has to answer, then it's his turn to ask you a question. It's fun! Many times normal conversation will start out of one of the questions. If that awkward silence happens again just start the game over with another question.

Should I make him get the door?

You should never make him do anything. You should allow him to get the door. You need to be a lady in order for him to be a gentleman. Some guys need a little more prompting than others on being gentlemen. So wait patiently until he opens the door. He'll get the message.

Where should I sit in the car?

Since you've allowed him to open the car door for you, go ahead and sit right there in the passenger seat. I always giggle when I see a couple driving along with the girl sitting so close to the guy that he can hardly drive. But there is a compromise. Maybe after you've gone out with him for a while you will feel comfortable sitting closer to him in the car, but don't rush it on the first date. Enjoy the evening. Don't do anything you don't feel comfortable about.

What if I make a fool of myself?

What qualifies as making a fool of yourself? Spilling something on yourself? Tripping? Having a booger hanging out of your nose? These situations can all be very embarrassing, but at the same time they happen to everyone. Don't make a bigger deal out of something than it is. If you spill something, just excuse yourself, go to the ladies' room, and clean up as best you can. If you don't make a big deal out of it, the guy probably won't either. If he does think less of you, then I would question how terrific he is in the first place. Who did he think he was taking out, anyway? Miss Perfect? He could just as easily have made a fool of himself.

A close friend of mine took a girl out and wasn't

looking when he closed her car door. He accidentally slammed it on her hand. So they spent the rest of the evening in the hospital getting her hand X-rayed! Now that's embarrassing!

But we're all human. So don't worry about making mistakes. Just be yourself. Dating is supposed to be fun!

2 Corinthians 6:14—"Do not be yoked together with unbelievers. For what do righteousnes and wickedness have in common? Or what fellowship can light have with darkness?" *This verse emphasizes the vast difference between a Christian and a non-Christian. It is important to date someone with whom you have things in common. As Christians we really don't have much in common with unbelievers.*

1 Corinthians 10:31—"So whether you eat or drink or whatever you do, do it all for the glory of God." *No matter what you do in life—whether it be dating the guy next door or becoming President of the United States—do it all for the glory of God.*

Purity

My Little Sisters,

Praise the Lord for His creation of the opposite sex! Wow! He knew what He was doing when He made us male and female! The differences can be fun stuff.

There is no reason for you to ever feel guilty about your feelings towards a guy or the physical desires you have. God made you 100 percent human and those feelings are part of being human. But He does tell us that the fulfillment of those desires is to be saved for marriage. As a young woman, you need to start thinking about where to draw the line in the area of physical contact with guys. You need to be aware of your limits and how much you can handle.

Hand Holding

You're at a football game and the most wonderful guy in the world is sitting next to you. You have liked him forever, and his best friend just told you that he likes you too.

He moves over closer to you on the bench. He's sort of nervous and jumpy, but slowly (and I do mean slowly) he gets hold of your hand. All of a sudden the sky opens up and one million angels begin singing and there are fireworks! In your mind

you tell yourself you'll never wash that hand again. This is the greatest thing in the world, and you can now die a happy woman.

A few minutes go by and then a half hour and then another hour. Your hands begin to sweat, soon a puddle of perspiration starts to form under the bench. Suddenly hand holding isn't as much fun as it was earlier.

Arm Around

Soon your friend begins to act kind of tired and gives a great big yawn. **Yawn!** He stretches his arms behind his back and then relaxes. Boom! What do you know? His arm accidentally lands around you! Again the sky opens up, angels sing, and there are fireworks. This is truly wonderful.

Hugging

Maybe the guy asks you out for an official date. When he walks you to the door, things seem a little awkward and you're dying to know what's going to happen next. Then it happens. He hugs you! Ahhhhhh! How wonderful. Go ahead, hug back, it's neat.

Kissing

Whoa, babes! Now we get into the big time. In this case let's define kissing as just a quick little kiss. Just a peck. You know, the kind you give your grandmother. Wheeeeee! Smack!

My suggestion is that you be very selective about whom you kiss. Kissing is fun stuff, but if you kiss *just any guy then how do you show the one you really like that he is special? Save your kisses for the special guys.*

French Kissing

Wow! The international stuff. Let's define this as kissing with your mouth open and playing tongue tag. Oops! You're it!

Petting

This is not the same as you do to your dog or cat. Petting is when hands start doing some searching in places where they should not be. You know, the parts your bathing suit covers up. This is also called foreplay and is designed to lead to sexual intercourse.

Sexual Intercourse

The "Big I," IT, going all the way. Sexual intercourse is the joining of a man and woman through the act of sex. Sounds vague and scientific, doesn't it? What it really is, is a wonderful creation by God to unite a husband and wife in an expression of love. I stress the words husband and wife *because that is who God made sex for.*

"So Jami, now that I know all this stuff, what do I do with it?"

Well, I'm glad you asked! Set a standard! Draw your line! Pick a limit! But do it now. Don't wait until you're stuck somewhere with a guy to start thinking about how you're going to handle the situation. Prepare yourself now.

I suggest that you draw your line somewhere near hugging and kissing. You may want to wait until your parents allow you to date before you start kissing and I don't mean right away or on the very first date. If you kiss a guy right away you've given as much as you're going to give before you get married. So save your kisses for a while.

The best kiss I've ever had came after I waited for what seemed to be an eternity. I had been dating Mark for about two months and had waited for so long for him to kiss me that I didn't think it was ever going to happen. Finally I gave up; this man was never going to kiss me. I invited him over for dinner one night and made Mexican food complete with onions. (Why not? He was never going to kiss me.) But what a sly fox he was. When dinner was over we went into the living room and Mark started a fire in the fireplace. At first I thought it was romantic, then I figured he must be cold. Boy, was I surprised when he put his arm around me and gave me the most romantic, special kiss in the whole world. Let me tell you, I was glad I waited.

I strongly recommend that you draw your line at kissing. If you go past that, you're playing with fire and are headed for trouble. You may find yourself in a situation where even though you want to stop, your hormones want to keep going. Anything after kissing is known as foreplay and leads to intercourse. I've come to the conclusion that petting is like a "preview of coming attractions" at the movies. When I see a good preview I think, "Wow, that looks like a great movie! I want to see the whole thing!" That's a little like petting. You get a little and you want the whole thing!

We are surrounded by a society that tells us to "go for the gusto" and to get all we can. So why shouldn't we keep going when it comes to sex? I'll tell you why! Because God doesn't want us to. His Word tells us to flee from youthful lust and to abstain from sexual immorality. We should stop because **God wants us to stop!** Sex is to be saved for marriage. Believe it or not, becoming involved in premarital sex is one of the most destructive things you can do to yourself and to a relationship. At your age, the guy you date probably won't end up as your husband. So when you are no longer dating him what you will have left is a friendship. During your dating time you need to keep asking yourself, "How will this affect our friendship later on?" Don't do things that are going to hurt that friendship. Sex will definitely hurt it.

You may think that just because I'm writing this book I must be a saint. Guess again! I'm no different than you are. I have considered giving in to temptation several times, but I haven't done it. God tells us that we will never be tempted beyond what we can handle. And He promises to give us His strength to say no to temptation. For our part we need to stay away from trouble situations in order to avoid being tempted. So don't be alone with a guy in a situation where the temptation can be unbearable. Be sure to spend time with guys who want only the best for you. And think about good and pure things instead of filling your mind with sexually suggestive movies or books. If you do find yourself in a tempting situation, turn around and run the other way! Get out before you allow yourself to get in trouble.

By the way, physical contact, even as little as hand holding, communicates a message. It suggests to the other person that you like him in a special way and that there is a certain amount of commitment or affection between you. Don't lead on a guy in whom you aren't interested by hugging and kissing just because you want to hug and kiss. Ask yourself a few questions when you start spending a lot of time with a guy. Am I being honest with him about my feelings when I let him touch me? Do I really like him or do I just want to go out with someone . . . anyone?

Try to picture a gift that is beautifully wrapped with colorful paper, ribbons, and lace. Your purity is like that precious gift. Just as you wouldn't consider handing a gift to a perfect stranger, why would you consider kissing someone you hardly know? And just as you wouldn't consider setting a beautiful gift in front of a pig knowing that he'd just roll it through the mud, why would you date a guy who has a bad reputation?

Someday the most wonderful man in the world is going to come into your life and the precious gift of your purity will be just for him. You're going to be anxious to give it to him, too. But there is a timeliness to the gift. Let me illustrate my point with a little story . . . .

When I was a little girl, Christmas was my

favorite holiday. I would come home from school each day before Christmas and count all the packages with my name on them. On Christmas Day I would get up at four in the morning and beg my mom to let me open my presents. She'd send me back to bed and we'd go through the same routine at 5:00 A.M. and 6:00 A.M. One year I couldn't wait to find out what I was getting for Christmas. So before my mom even had a chance to wrap the gifts, I sneaked into her room and peeked in the closet. I found all of my gifts and they were perfect! Just for me—right size, right color. My mom had great taste. Well, Christmas Day came around and I wasn't as excited as usual. I already knew what I was getting. I didn't get up at 4:00, 5:00, or 6:00 A.M. Everybody else was thrilled by the surprise of the wonderful gifts they received, but I already knew what I was getting, so it wasn't as much fun for me. My presents were still great, but because I didn't wait until the right time to open them they were less special.

In the same way, when that extra-special man comes along you are going to be dying to give him your gift. But that gift will only be at its very best when it's given at the right time, and that is on the day you are married.

Plan ahead. Set your standards now. Don't wait until it's too late. Don't be stuck with a gift that is already opened and used. And cherish and guard your gift until the time is right.

Jami

Philippians 4:8—"Finally, brothers, whatever is true, whatever is noble, whatever is right, whatever is pure, whatever is lovely, whatever is admirable—if anything is excellent or praiseworthy—think about such things." *Dwell on the things that God would have you think about. That will keep your mind off things that might tempt you to do wrong.*

2 Timothy 2:22—"Flee the evil desires of youth, and pursue righteousness, faith, love and peace, along with those who call on the Lord out of a pure heart." *If you find yourself caught in a tempting situation then flee from it and pursue after things of the Lord.*

1 Corinthians 10:13—"No temptation has seized you except what is common to man. And God is faithful; he will not let you be tempted beyond what you can bear. But when you are tempted, he will provide a way out so that you can stand up under it." *God never allows us to be tempted beyond what we can handle; He provides a way to escape. It is through His strength that we are able to say no and turn away from temptation.*

1 John 1:9—"If we confess our sins, he is faithful and just and will forgive us our sins and purify us from all unrighteousness." *There may be times when you go too far and give in to temptation. All you need to do is to turn to God and ask for His forgiveness. He forgives you and cleanses you so that in His eyes you are as white as snow.*

Breaking Up

My Little Sisters,

I wish I could be there to pass the Kleenex and help wipe the tears every time a boy breaks your heart. I've had my share of broken hearts, too. Maybe some day I will write a book called "Scar Wars." Let me share a few of my wounds with you.

I dated a guy once who absolutely swept me off my feet. We dated steadily for about a month and then I went to counsel at camp for a week. After the week was over he came to pick me up, and as we were driving home he told me he had gone out with another girl. That hurt badly enough, but then he told me that she was a girl I had introduced him to. I wanted to rip her eyes out (in Christian love, of course)!

Another guy I dated on and off for about 10 months worked at the camp where I counseled each summer. The one time we were at camp together he chose to ignore me the whole week. I don't mind telling you, I was mad! Being the brave person I am, however, I left a note on his car telling him never to call me again. (Really brave, huh?)

Only a couple of months ago I broke up with the best boyfriend I've ever had. We dated for almost three years. Oh, the beautiful, romantic, mushy stories I could tell you! But we had very different hopes and expectations for our lives. I found myself trying to force him to live up to my expectations for what I wanted instead of letting him be who he wanted to be. He wasn't happy and neither was I. So we had to change our boyfriend/girl friend relationship to one of friendship out of respect for one another.

As traumatic as those breakups were at the time, they all turned out well. The guy who dumped me for another girl wrote to me years later to apologize and to tell me what a valuable person I was and how much my friendship meant to him. The guy who ignored me at camp talked to me a year later and we buried the hatchet. We are very close friends now. As for the best boyfriend I ever had, he is still a very dear and close friend and we still date each other once in a while.

I told you in another letter that I was engaged once. I was terribly hurt and bitter when the engagement was broken and never wanted to talk to the guy again. Well, after seven years went by I began to wonder what ever happened to him, so I tracked him down by phone. We talked for an hour about old times and caught up on details of the last seven years. After all that time we have finally begun to reconstruct a very valuable friendship.

When each of those breakups first occurred I thought I would die. I wanted the world to stop so that I could concentrate on feeling sorry for myself and cry my eyes out. But the world never stopped for me and life went on.

How about you? What do you do when a guy

breaks up with you? If you're normal, you cry a lot. Do you know what I say to that? Go ahead and cry good and hard. Get it all out. Being rejected hurts; you deserve a good cry. You may experience some other feelings too. You may become very bitter and hate guys altogether. I usually did. I'd hate the whole lot of them for about a day or two or until another cute one came along. You may feel like there will never again be anyone as wonderful as your boyfriend. I have felt that way often, but I have had to trust God. If God wants me to get married some day, He will have to bring along the right person for me, someone who will be better than all the others. You will have to trust God to do the same for you.

There are times when we are the ones who choose to break up a relationship. Yuk! I don't know of any girl who likes to break up with a guy, but sometimes you don't have any other choice. Here are two suggestions for making it easier. (Unfortunately, I mean easier for him. These suggestions won't make things easier for you, I'm afraid.) The first one is to put yourself in his shoes. How would you feel if he were breaking up with you? Would you want him to avoid you? Would you want him to have his friend tell you things were over? No. You would want him to tell you himself. And you would want him to tell you as soon as possible after he'd reached the decision. Put the guy's feelings first. He is going to hurt enough when you break up. Don't make it worse by putting it off or having someone else tell him.

The second suggestion is to be honest. Don't make up excuses about how you are planning to become a nun or join a convent. If you simply don't feel that he is your type, then tell him that. I beg you to be gentle. Sometimes the truth can be painful. Honesty is one thing, but giving a guy a list of his bad qualities and telling him that those are the reasons you're breaking up is quite another.

Often we feel that we have failed when a relationship doesn't work out. I think we look at a successful relationship as one that lasts forever and turns into marriage. But that perspective is unrealistic when it comes to dating. Hopefully we will only get married once. If we are to have more than one boyfriend in our lives then they can't all become our husbands. I think we should look at a successful relationship as one from which we learn more about ourselves, our likes and dislikes, our strong points and weaknesses, and what kind of guy suits us best. But most of all a successful relationship should also involve a successful friendship. It's hard to be friends when you first break up, but I hope that later down the line you will make every effort to include your old boyfriends in your list of friends (even if it takes seven years).

I think the line I always hated most from a guy was that he "just wanted to be friends." Sometimes I'd feel like I was having to settle for less than the best, but as I said in another chapter, friends are valuable. Boyfriends come and go, but friends can last forever.

What hurts most about breaking up is how we

feel about ourselves afterwards. It's common to feel ugly or worthless or that no one will ever love us again. That couldn't be further from the truth. None of us is really ugly as long as we are beautiful on the inside. None of us is worthless either. We are here on earth for a very special reason known only to God. I can't guarantee that there will be another boyfriend waiting for you right around the corner. But there is Someone waiting to pick up the pieces and wipe away the tears. That Someone is God. He is always there. And He loves you just the way you are. No one will ever be able to take that away from you, either. Nothing can separate you from the love of God. He is yours forever.

Romans 8:28—"And we know that in all things God works for the good of those who love him, who have been called according to his purpose." *Believe it or not, God can bring good out of something as awful as breaking up. He may teach you a new lesson or simply to have faith in Him through tough experiences.*

Romans 8:38—"For I am convinced that nothing can ever separate us from his love. Death can't, and life can't. The angels won't, and all the powers of hell itself cannot keep God's love away" (TLB). *God is always there to love you. Nothing can ever take that love away.*

Psalm 34:18—"The Lord is close to the brokenhearted and saves those who are crushed in spirit." *When you hurt so bad inside that you think your heart is breaking, turn to God. He is there to help you, love you, and take care of you.*

Speech

My Little Sisters,

I have a great deal of growing up to do when it comes to the area of speech. The way I talk about others is at times the pits. I love knowing secrets that are none of my business, and, worse yet, passing them on. That's known as gossiping, and the Bible tells us that it is a sin. So as I write to you, I am still learning.

The way we talk reflects the condition of our hearts. When we say kind and loving things our hearts are probably full of kindness and consideration. But when we use cruel words, they reveal hearts that are filled with poison. How many times have you wished you hadn't said what you did? Or you just couldn't believe the words that suddenly flew out of your mouth uncontrollably? My list of the times that has happened is endless. There have been so many thousands of times I wish I had just kept my mouth shut.

Anger

I've never been one to lose my temper and tell someone off face-to-face. But boy oh boy, when I talk to people about someone else or something that makes me angry I can be cruel-hearted and mean. I'm so afraid to tell someone off directly that I'll tell everyone else about it. I'll even lie in bed at night and think of mean things to say, but I'll never say them to that person. (And you thought you were the only one who did that!) So what good does all that do? None! Not an ounce of good.

Getting angry about something usually doesn't solve anything. But dealing with the problem does. Instead of letting your anger grow, try to find a solution to the problem. Anger is a human emotion that is not bad. But how we express anger can be very harmful to others and ourselves. Jesus got mad only a few times, and His kind of anger was righteous anger. He was angry because merchants were abusing His Father's house and trying to make a profit inside the Temple. (Kind of like having K-Mart come to your church to sell salvation!) Unfortunately, our anger usually isn't the righteous kind. We get angry because someone has mistreated us or because we are jealous. It is a very self-centered and selfish anger.

How should we deal with anger? Well, I'm the type of person who has to wait a while to let my anger cool down, or I'm sure to say something I'll regret later. Some people count to 10 before they react. It is usually wisest for me to count to one million before I deal with the situation. It gives me plenty of time to look at the options and be objective.

It is important to deal with a frustrating situation sooner or later. Many people just let things pass and think they will forget all about them. But what happens is that the tension within builds up more and more until they explode. If you deal with a problem while it is still minor it never has the chance to get blown out of proportion. By dealing with the situation I don't mean running up to a person and telling her that she really ticked you off yesterday and then storming away in a huff. Look at the whole situation. Maybe the person who made you angry didn't really mean what she said, or maybe she just had a bad day herself. You will keep more friends if you approach them in a kind and loving way and let them know that you were hurt by something they said or did. And be sure to forgive the person who made you mad even if she doesn't ask for forgiveness.

Lying

Not many of us would consider ourselves liars. But we all stretch the truth from time to time or leave out certain incriminating details of a story. I have a friend who stretches the truth a lot! There is no way she could have done all the things she claims to have done. Some of her friends have found out that her exaggerations are false and they no longer believe everything she tells them. That's sad, because the reason she exaggerates is to get people to like her. But when they find out that she has stretched the truth they don't respect her.

We exaggerate to make ourselves look special and important. But if the people around us don't love us for what we truly are, then their love isn't worth much. More important, we need to love and accept ourselves just as we are. Then we won't need to stretch the truth to gain the acceptance and love of others.

The problem of lying, however, is a bit different. We lie to keep ourselves out of trouble. We don't like to admit it when we've done wrong, so we lie. But guess what! Our lies always catch up to us.

Just today my boss told me that he heard I made a mess and didn't clean it up. It would have been so easy to tell him that someone else was supposed to have done it, but I didn't. "Oops," I said, "I'm sorry. I forgot all about it. I'll try not to do it again." He shrugged his shoulders and said, "No big deal," and it was over.

What if I had lied to my boss? He would have gone back to the other people and told them they were wrong. No matter what he believed, those people would have known I had lied. It seems that whenever you lie you have to tell a few more lies to support the first one. Here's a hint: Don't even start with one lie. When you've done wrong, be big enough to admit it and then apologize.

Cussing

Swearing or using cuss words is kind of a strange thing. Many cuss words mean the same thing as clean words. So big deal, if they both mean the same thing, then what's the difference if we use cuss words or not? It's really hard to say. Some people are offended by certain words. Around my mom's house we were never allowed to say "Shut up." Some big cuss word, huh? But my mom couldn't stand hearing people talk to each other with such disrespect. In our society certain words and phrases are considered strong or harsh. They are what you might call ugly words. You know, the kind of language that you would hear in a stereotypical men's locker room or from a truck driver, or even from a bunch of girls. They are words used by people who often don't care what other people think of them, or because they are undisciplined and uncreative in their expressions.

As Christians we should care very much what people think of us. How will non-Christians know that we are different when we talk like they do and can't control those ugly words that come out of our mouths? Junior competition sports are common here in Southern California. When people make mistakes during the game they lose their tempers and cuss. No control. What if all Christian players responded the same as non-Christians? What about trying to be like Christ? What about using God's strength to control our tongues?

Teasing

When I like people or try to make people feel like part of the group I usually tease them. But it's a friendly kind of teasing. Unfortunately, many kids are not known for their friendly kind of teasing. I used to ride the bus to school. One day a bunch of the kids started picking on a girl sitting near me. She had not said or done anything to warrant that kind of treatment. I felt sorry for her and told her to just ignore them. I'm sure she's forgotten all about the incident. But I have another friend who was in a similar situation and who never forgot. A group of us went for a little hike at camp. Only two guys were with us, and the big guy, Rob, kept picking on the little one, Brad. I finally got tired of Rob's teasing and told him to knock it off. Well, I forgot all about the episode, but years later when I was 21 I got a call one night from Brad. I hadn't seen him since we were in junior high, but he got my phone number from a mutual friend and called me to thank me for sticking up for him against Rob. He wanted to repay me by taking me out to dinner. Pretty neat, huh?

Most people rip on others to make themselves feel big and tough. Do you want to have more friends? Then help those around you feel good about themselves by giving them compliments instead of teasing them about their bad points. Stick up for them when the local bully starts picking on them. Who knows, maybe when you're 21 you'll get a call from a long-lost friend who just wants to say thanks.

Gossip

"Did you hear . . . " "Guess what happened to . . . " "And then she said . . . " Sound familiar? If you know me it does. No matter how much I want to control my tongue, such words find their way out of my mouth before I know it. Most people love gossip. They love to hear it and they love to tell it. But have you ever noticed how a rumor changes as it travels?

"Hey, did you hear that John and Sharon went to church together?"

"You'll never guess who's dating! Sharon and John!"

"I heard John asked Sharon to go steady."

"Guess what! John asked Sharon to go steady and she turned him down flat!"

"Sharon asked John to get married. But he turned her down. I wonder if they have to get married!"

Poor John and Sharon. All they did was ride to church together because Sharon's car ran out of gas. But in our joy of passing on juicy information the story gets bigger and bigger and bigger. How would you feel if you were the one who started the rumor? Even worse, how would you feel if you were Sharon?

Gossip ruins friendships more quickly than anything else. When a friend tells you something and asks you to keep it a secret, what do you do? Do you run to the phone and call the newspaper to have it put on the front page? Or do you do as your friend asked and keep her secret? I encourage you to be someone whom your friends can trust. Learn to get control of your tongue and don't spread or start rumors.

One quick way to stop a rumor is to ask a few questions of the person who tells it to you. "Where did you hear that one? Do you mind if I tell the person who's being gossiped about that I heard it from you?"

Sometimes gossip can really ruin a person's reputation. I heard some really juicy stuff about one of the guys I work with at church. What I heard

91

made me lose respect for him, so I decided to ask him about it. It certainly was interesting to find out that none of what I heard about him was true. Don't believe everything you hear—especially when it's gossip!

In the last few months I've learned that I can control my tongue with very little effort if I put God in charge. I let Him take control. I have begun to read more from the Bible and to eliminate the use of one ugly word at a time from my vocabulary. It is amazing how quickly all the ugly words have disappeared and my temper has come under control.

You can do the same. Let God take charge. If you let His sweetness come into your heart then that sweetness will be what comes out of your mouth.

Jami

James 3:2—"We all stumble in many ways. If anyone is never at fault in what he says, he is a perfect man, able to keep his whole body in check." *The Bible tells us how hard it is to control the tongue. If we are able to control our tongues, good conduct will follow.*

Ephesians 4:25—"Therefore each of you must put off falsehood and speak truthfully to his neighbor, for we are all members of one body." *A falsehood is an exaggeration or allowing someone to believe something that isn't the whole truth. Be sure that when you tell a story you are telling the whole truth.*

Ephesians 5:4—"Dirty stories, foul talk and coarse jokes—these are not for you. Instead, remind each other of God's goodness and be thankful" (TLB). *God wants us to set a good example of what followers of Christ are like. He doesn't want us to get a reputation for having filthy mouths or always picking on others.*

Ephesians 4:26—"If you are angry, don't sin by nursing your grudge. Don't let the sun go down with you still angry—get over it quickly" (TLB). *If someone else has been wronged, we are right to be angry. But we should not let that anger fester inside us for long. God says to deal with it the very same day.*

Parents

My Little Sisters,

I've been wanting to write this letter to you for a long, long time. But I have felt that I couldn't tell you to do things that I wasn't doing myself. I have not always been the loving daughter that I should have been. But God has finally taken me to a point in my life where He has taught me some valuable lessons that I can share with you. They have not been learned without pain. You'll understand what I mean when you're finished with this letter.

Parents are a funny breed. They wear clothes that young people wouldn't be caught dead in, they don't have a clue about what the real world is like because they're always living in the past, they've forgotten what it's like to be young, and they have a knack for saying the wrong things at the wrong time. Let's face it! You'd rather be caught dead than be seen in public with them.

Does that sound like your feelings about your folks? Most kids feel that way. I know I did. Kids who don't are an exception (and I hope their parents appreciate it). I loved my parents while I was growing up, but I didn't want to be their little girl forever. The time I decided to claim my independence, meet the world head on, and be my own person was about the same time I quit wanting to be seen with my parents. I felt that they gave me a bad image, cramped my style, so to speak. I was only 12 years old at the time. So you can see how easy it was for them to see things differently than I did.

That's probably what you're going through right now. You want to be independent and grown up. But in your parents' eyes you've only started to grow up. Parents understand that growing up doesn't happen overnight and that it is a long, slow process. They are standing by to help. So listen to their words and heed their advice. It may not make any sense to you now, but as you mature you'll discover that they really knew what they were talking about.

The thing that used to bug me the most about my parents when I was younger was that they never treated my brother, my sister, and me the same way. My sister got to do everything that I couldn't do, and my little brother got away with murder. There were times that I thought my parents were off their ever-lovin' rockers. How could they raise three kids from the same family so cotton-pickin' differently?

I'll tell you how. Somewhere along the line they must have read Proverbs 22:6—"Train a child in the way he should go, and when he is old he will not turn from it." Did you catch that? It actually says to treat each child as an individual. My big sister was completely different than I was. Our needs varied, so we had to be treated differently. And what would have happened if my parents had raised my brother just as they did their daughters? He would have

gotten dolls for Christmas and a new dress each
Easter. Not only were our physical needs different
but so were our mental needs. My sister got good
grades in school; mine were average. So I needed to
study more, and that meant that Mom had to
pressure me into doing homework. My sister was
neat and tidy; my room was a mess. So Mom was
always nagging me to clean it up. As I look back on
it now, it was really no big deal. In some areas I
needed more discipline, in other areas my brother
and sister did.

Next time your parents treat you differently from
your brother or sister remember that they are trying
to raise individuals, not clones. Believe it or not,
your parents are doing what they believe is the very
best for you. "But Jami, you ought to hear some of
the stupid rules they place on me. They don't trust
me with anything!" I felt the same way. We had a
rule as I was growing up that I couldn't go anywhere
with a guy in a van. How dumb! What difference
does the kind of car make? I thought that had to be
the stupidest rule in the entire world—until they let
me go out with a guy who drove a van! I found out
very quickly that they had worried for the right
reason and that they had set a good rule.

God has given you a set of parents to respect
and obey. He hand-picked them. This doesn't
exclude stepparents either. God has you right where
He wants you, and He's big enough to keep
everything in control. You can learn and grow up to
be a fine adult if you listen closely to what your
parents tell you. God is using them to help you

become the person He wants you to become.

The first commandment in the Bible with a promise attached says, "Honor your father and mother . . . that it may go well with you" (Eph. 6:2,3). Your life will be better if you listen to your folks.

The Bible tells parents that if they spare the rod they'll spoil the child. I now understand that Mom did her very best to see that I didn't grow up to be a spoiled-rotten brat. Your parents are probably trying to help you become a terrific adult. Going through all of the growing up it takes to get there can be rough, though. They may seem to be your worst enemies, but they're not. The Bible says to listen to their wise words and not stray from their teaching. Would you hate me too much if I told you that parents usually know best? They were kids once too and can remember the pains and mistakes they went through while growing up. They see things from a better perspective.

When I was about five, my mom had a friend over for lunch. She brought along her son, Jimmy John. I wanted to have fun playing outside with Jimmy John. But it was time for my nap and my mom sent me to my room to lie down instead. Well, I was one furious little five-year-old. I decided to get back at my mom. I found a box of crayons and proceeded to draw a picture on the wall. I have no idea what I drew, but I have a feeling it was of my mom and it wasn't very pretty.

When I was done with the picture I fell asleep and forgot all about it. My mom wandered into my room later on and saw it. "Jami," she asked, "did you draw this picture on the wall?"

I looked at her with my big green eyes and said, "No."

"Then who did?" she asked.

I shrugged my shoulders and said, "I don't know."

Well, she knew who did it and after she spanked me, she handed me a can of Comet and made me clean the wall. That was probably worse than the spanking because that dumb crayon drawing wouldn't come off. The moral of this story is that I now know better than to draw on walls. Simple lesson, right? Well, I have a friend who has yet to learn that same lesson. Whenever he comes over he writes on stuff all over my house. He writes on several pages of my favorite stationery, on the back of my name badge for work, and so on and so on. Maybe I should hand him a bottle of Comet and teach him not to ruin other people's property since his parents never did.

My mom is a beautiful woman inside and out. But I didn't always see it that way. When I was little I had an odd notion that beautiful women were mean, wicked, and cruel. Since my mom did all the disciplining in our house, I figured she was no exception. She let me have it on the rump more than once with her hand or the fly swatter. I thought she was being mean. She was really being the most loving mother she could be.

Girls, I took my mom for granted up until I was 21 years old. I had no idea how wonderful she was until I moved out on my own. When I lived with her I hated the discipline and I never noticed the loving things she did for me. She was the tooth fairy, the one who bought all of my Christmas and birthday presents, and the one who sewed clothes for me and taught me how to sew. More than once she spent money on her children that she could have used for herself. She told me about "the birds and the bees," took me to church, cleaned my room while I was at camp, and tried her hardest to have daily devotions with me. She consoled me during the years I didn't make it as a cheerleader and took time off work to come watch me the year I did. She taught me how to handle money and encouraged me to go to college. She continues to remind me that I am a very special woman.

My mom is my very best friend. On the day I finally get married I hope that she will be the one to walk me down the aisle to give me away. My mom and I have had some terribly hard times between us. There were times when we just couldn't see eye to eye.

As I began to grow into a young woman I started having ideas and opinions of my own. That was hard on my mom because she was used to her ideas being accepted as best. But unlike some parents, she let her children form their own opinions rather than forcing her ideas on them. Some parents can't do that and their relationships with their children suffer for it. My mother knew what she was doing as a parent, but I was too shortsighted to appreciate her at the time. Do you appreciate your parents for doing a good job of raising you? Tell them so. Don't wait until you're 21 to figure it out like I did.

Now I want to tell you about my father. When I was young my dad said yes to everything—ice cream, candy, and a new Barbie doll. I knew that if Mom said no then I could go to Dad; he was sure to say yes. As I grew up my dad spent less and less time around the house. He was usually at work or coaching a little kids' football team. It didn't really bother my sister and brother and me not to have him around because it wasn't anything special when he was there.

When I was about 16 my parents divorced. Dad moved to a nearby city so that we were still able to see him once in a while. But soon he developed a drinking problem, and it was difficult to be with him. We would make plans to see each other for birthdays and holidays but he would always cancel. My father had become an alcoholic, and I have to admit, I really didn't want to see him.

Dad was admitted to the hospital a couple of times because of his drinking, but I never knew how seriously ill he was. He would quit drinking for a while and then start up again.

One day I got a call from a friend of his who said that Dad had been in the hospital for almost a week and that his condition had become so grave that a family member should be contacted. I was considered Dad's next of kin, so I was the one contacted.

As I drove to the hospital all I could think of was how angry I was that he had ended up in the hospital again. But when I walked into his room and saw Dad sleeping, with all kinds of tubes running in and out of him, I was so shocked that I turned around and left the room until I could stop crying. When I came back in, I talked to some of his roommates, and Dad didn't even open his eyes to see who it was. He knew. He just said, "Hi, Squirt."

We made small talk for a while and then it was time for me to go. Before I left, I kissed his forehead and told him I loved him and that I was always there if he needed me. That was the last time I ever got to talk to my father, because soon after that he went into a coma and then died. I may not have been the best daughter in the world and Dad may not have been the best father, but I'm so thankful that God gave me that final chance to express my love to Dad.

It would be wonderful to have a perfect set of parents. But no one is perfect. Sadly enough, there are family situations that are so difficult that the children are faced with violent and sometimes dangerous circumstances. There isn't only one answer to these problems. If you or a friend are dealing with a problem like this, I recommend that you seek the counsel of your youth pastor or a school counselor. They will be able to give you advice based on your individual circumstances.

When parents behave irrationally and become violent in the treatment of their own children, it is likely that those kids will have feelings of hatred or anger toward their parents. Those kinds of feelings cause a great deal of confusion. But even God hates violent behavior against an innocent person. It is okay to hate the sinful actions of parents, but you *must continue to love them as people.*

Do your parents know that you love them? Do you ever tell them? What if something were suddenly to happen to your mother or father— would they know that you love them? Do me a favor, put this book down and go tell your parents that you love them. Tell them that you care. Perhaps you've never heard your parents say they love you, but that's no excuse to keep you from expressing your love to them. It's easy to love a parent who is like my mom, not so easy to love one like my dad. But God wants us to love and honor our parents regardless of the circumstances.

Jami

Ephesians 6:1-3—"Children, obey your parents in the Lord, for this is right. 'Honor your father and mother'—which is the first commandment with a promise—'that it may go well with you and that you may enjoy long life on the earth.'" *God wants us to obey our parents so that our lives will be more full and rewarding. Parents give wise advice that makes life easier.*

Proverbs 1:8-9—"Listen, my son, to your father's instruction and do not forsake your mother's teaching. They will be a garland to grace your head and a chain to adorn your neck." *The instruction and teaching that parents give are like jewels to be proudly worn. They are beautiful and valuable words.*

Brothers and Sisters

My Little Sisters,

When it comes to the subject of brothers and sisters we all feel pretty much the same: we can't stand them. Well, most of the time we can't stand them. Sometimes they're all right, but not often enough.

My sister Lee Ann is two years older than I am, and when we were younger she never let me forget it. See if those of you with older sisters can relate to any of this . . . . Lee Ann always got to do everything before I did. She got to shave her legs, wear nylons, date, stay out late, and go to boy/girl parties before I did. That used to make me so mad; it seemed so unfair. But just imagine if it had been the other way around. What if we were always allowed to do the same things at the same time? That wouldn't have been very fair to Lee Ann, since she was two years older than I was. But I was too selfish to see things that way.

My sister couldn't stand me. I can't say that I blame her much now because I was the world's biggest tattletale. I told on everything she did. Everything! My mom would come home from work and I would immediately start rattling off all the mean things Lee Ann had done that day. I tattled so much that all I had to do was call for my mom in my tattling tone of voice and from across the house she would tell my sister to leave me alone. Lee Ann and I disliked each other so much that we were convinced that we'd hate each other for the rest of our lives. My mom used to tell us that we would grow up to be best friends some day. We never believed her—until we grew up.

After my mom, my sister is my next best friend. When we reached college age and didn't have dates on Saturday night we would stay home and eat junk food and watch TV together. We got into the habit of going shopping together on the weekends. Now that Lee Ann lives across the country from me we can't spend much time together. I miss her on weekend afternoons that seem perfect for a shopping trip with my big sis. And holidays just aren't holidays without her. When our dad died she was the only one I could turn to who could understand my pain. So she lent me her shoulder and I cried and cried. She never told me to stop. She just let me be me. We call each other as often as we can, and it always seems that just when I'm thinking of her, Lee Ann will call me.

What bothers me is the fact that I had a best friend living with me until I became a young adult and I never took advantage of the situation. Instead, I tattled and picked on her. Girls, don't let that friend who lives right in your house get away before you start to treat her with the same kindness that you would give to any of your school friends.

The day before my fifth birthday Mom informed me that we would have to cancel my birthday party because she was going to the hospital to have a baby. I didn't like the idea! I wanted to have my birthday party . . . but my little brother wouldn't wait. A few days later mom returned home with a pink little baby named Brett. At first I didn't like him much. All he did was cry, eat, and make a mess in his diapers. But when he was two years old I thought he was the cutest little boy in the whole world. Lee Ann and I would compete for his attention.

As Brett and I grew up we had less and less in common. We had different feelings about family, school, and friendships. There always seemed to be a bit of an age gap between us. Brett wasn't out of elementary school when our parents divorced and we were never really sure if he understood what was going on in the family. He grew up in a completely different family atmosphere than Lee Ann and I did. He developed a different set of values and priorities than we did.

It has always been hard for me to accept my brother for who he is, but finally, at age 26, I'm learning to love Brett for who he is instead of who I think he should be.

Often we get afraid that our family members will embarrass us in front of our friends. They know us better than anyone else does, so they have incriminating information to use against us. But deep down we know that they probably care about us and understand us more than anyone else does. We are anxious to make things perfect for our friends and boyfriends, yet we talk to our brothers and sisters as though they were dirt, and we treat them the same way. But they are far more important than most friends or boyfriends we'll ever have.

You'll make a number of friends during your lifetime, but you'll never be able to replace your brothers and sisters. Start treating your brothers and sisters as if they were special instead of second-rate.

Jami

Proverbs 17:17—"A friend loves at all times, and a brother is born for adversity." *Friends are wonderful to have, but brothers and sisters can be even better because they will be there to help when things go wrong. Are you that kind of a sister?*

Going Steady with God

Hi, My Little Sisters,

I'll bet you think that a title like "Going Steady with God" is a strange name for one of my letters to you. But there is a reason, really.

When I was in junior and senior high school, going steady was a big deal. It meant that you were committed to a relationship and that you didn't date anyone but your steady. The two of your talked a lot on the phone, laughed together, were serious with each other, and were almost always together.

That's why I think my relationship with God is like going steady. We are committed to a relationship with one another. He has promised never to leave me, and I don't place anyone above Him. We talk to each other a lot. He talks to me through His written Word, the Bible, and I talk to Him in prayer. We laugh together; I know that He must giggle with me when I'm being silly, because He's the One who gave me my sense of humor. And we can be very serious, too. I turn to Him whenever I hurt or whenever I'm concerned about something, and He's always there to listen. Best of all, we are always together. No matter where I am or who I'm with, God is right there with me. That is very special to me.

God is waiting to have that kind of relationship

with you. He wants it so much that He sent His Son, Jesus, to the world so that you could be united with God. But in order for that to happen, Jesus had to die. You see, God is perfect, and because we've all sinned, we are separated from God. Our punishment for our sin was to be separation from God and death, until Jesus came to earth to die in our place. He was human and experienced all the trials and temptations that we do. The only difference is that He never sinned. He didn't have to die, but voluntarily chose to do so for you and me. Then He rose from the dead and returned to heaven to prepare an eternal home for us. Because of all that Jesus did, we no longer have to pay the punishment of sin. When we die we can join God in heaven forever. All we have to do is to believe that Jesus died for our sins, pray to Him and tell Him we want to accept His gift of eternal life, and then live according to what He says.

"But Jami, how do I know what God is saying? He doesn't talk to us today!" Oh, but He does! He gave us His written Word, the Bible. Through it He tells us everything we need to know. So you should study what He has to say, as if it were a letter written just for you. Do it every day. Start in the New Testament. (The book of James can give you some practical help in living as a Christian.) Read a little bit, then paraphrase it (write down in your own words what it says). After that, be specific. Write down what it says directly to you. How does it apply to your life? Use what you learn!

How do you feel when you're talking to a friend

and she doesn't say anything in response? Pretty dull, huh? You want to know how she's doing and how she feels. God is the same way. He wants us to talk to Him. He wants us to tell Him everything. He cares. So talk to Him. How? Through prayer. Don't be shy. You don't have to use big fancy words. Talk to Him as you would to a friend. He wants to be your best friend. Sometimes I write letters to Him just like I'm writing to you. It's fun! It's a different way of communicating with Him.

God wants to go steady with you. He wants to be your best friend, but it takes two to have a relationship.

There have been times in my life when I allowed myself to become too busy and preoccupied to remember to maintain my part of my friendship with God. But He never forgot me. He just waited for me to slow down enough to spend time with Him. God is waiting for you.

When I was in college a friend showed me a letter she had received. Its author remains anonymous, but it's a letter that Christ might send if He were to write to a friend. I have it taped to the inside of my Bible as a reminder of how much Christ wants to be my friend.

Dear Friend,

I just had to send a note to tell you how much I love you and care about you. I saw you yesterday as you were walking with your friends. I waited all day hoping you would want to talk with me also. As evening drew near, I gave you a sunset to close your day and a cool breeze to rest you. And I waited, but you never came. It hurt me, but I still love you because I am your friend.

I saw you fall asleep last night and longed to touch your brow. So I spilled moonlight on your pillow and your face. Again I waited, wanting to rush down so that we could talk. I have so many gifts for you. But you awakened late the next day and rushed off to work. My tears were in the rain.

Today you looked so sad, so all alone. It makes my heart ache because I understand. My friends let me down and hurt me so many times, too. But I love you. Oh, if you would only listen to me. I really love you. I try to tell you in the blue sky and in the quiet green grass. I whisper it in the leaves on the trees and breathe it in the colors of the flowers. I shout it to you in the mountain streams and give the birds love songs to sing. I clothe you with warm sunshine and perfume the air with nature's scents. My love for you is deeper than the oceans and bigger than the biggest want or need in your heart.

If you only knew how much I want to help you. I want you to meet my Father. He wants to help you, too. My Father is that way, you know. Just call me, ask me, talk with me. Please, please, don't forget me. I have so much to share with you. But I won't hassle you any further. You are free to call me. It's up to you. I'll wait because I love you.

Your friend,
Jesus

Romans 3:23—"For all have sinned and fall short of the glory of God."

Romans 6:23—"For the wages of sin is death . . . . "

Romans 5:8—"But God demonstrates His own love for us in this: While we were still sinners, Christ died for us."

John 14:6—"Jesus answered, 'I am the way and the truth and the life. No one comes to the Father except through me.'"

Ephesians 2:8,9—"For it is by grace you have been saved, through faith—and this not from yourselves, it is the gift of God—not by works, so that no one can boast."

Revelation 3:20—"Here I am! I stand at the door and knock. If anyone hears my voice and opens the door, I will come in . . . . "